SIMPLE DESIGNS

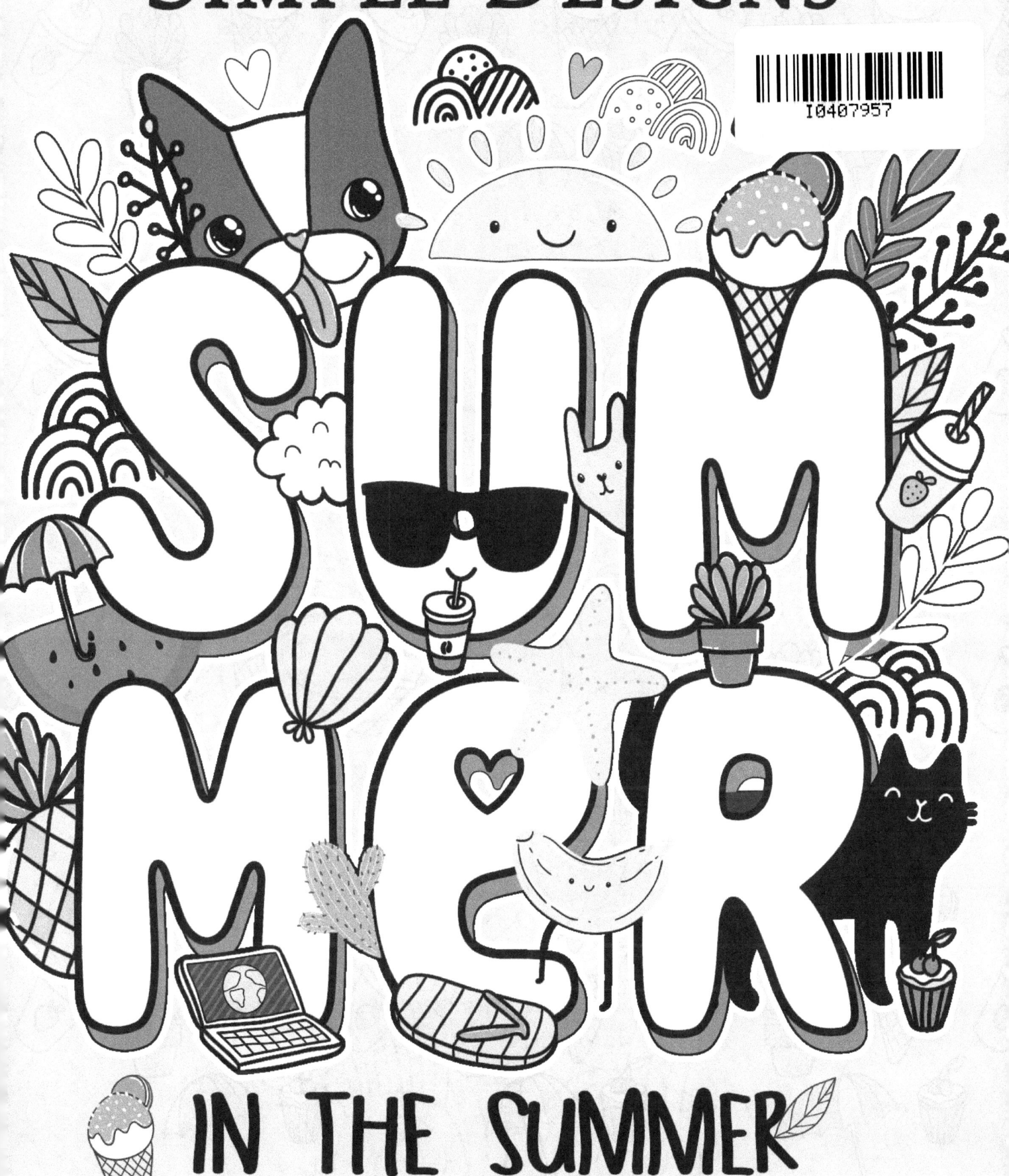

SUMMER

IN THE SUMMER
COLORING BOOKS FOR ADULTS
OCEAN, FLOWER AND CUTE DOODLE DESIGNS

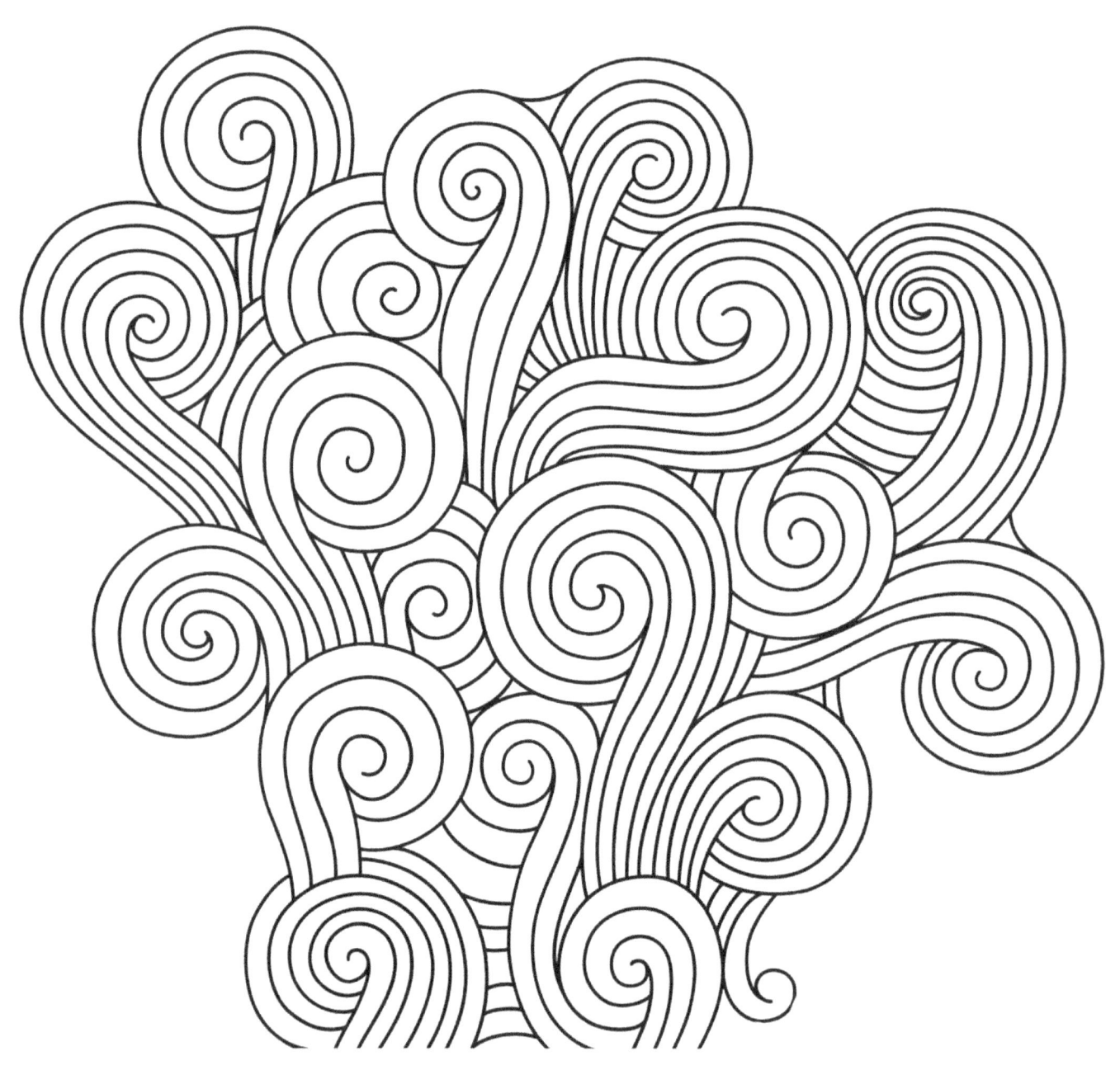

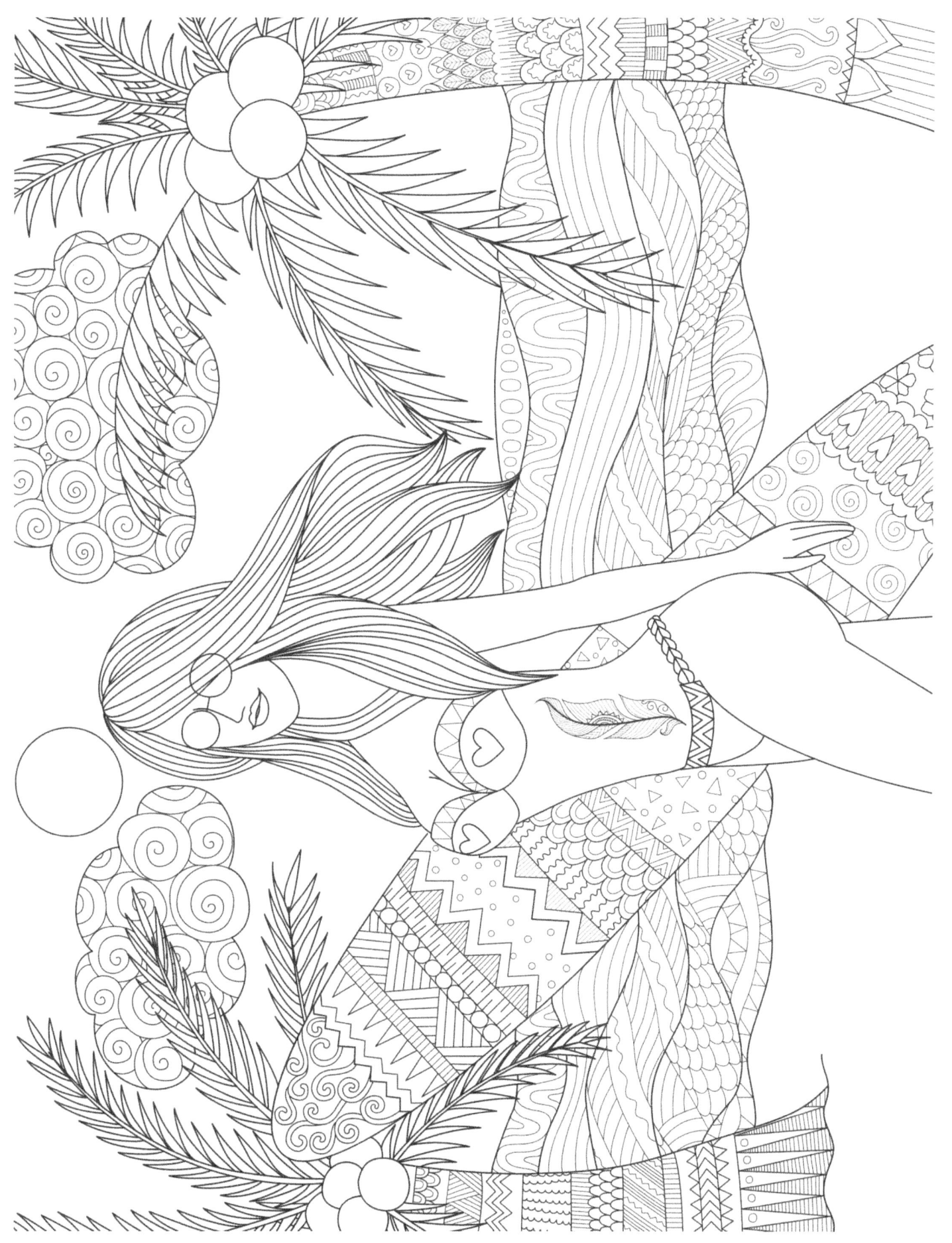

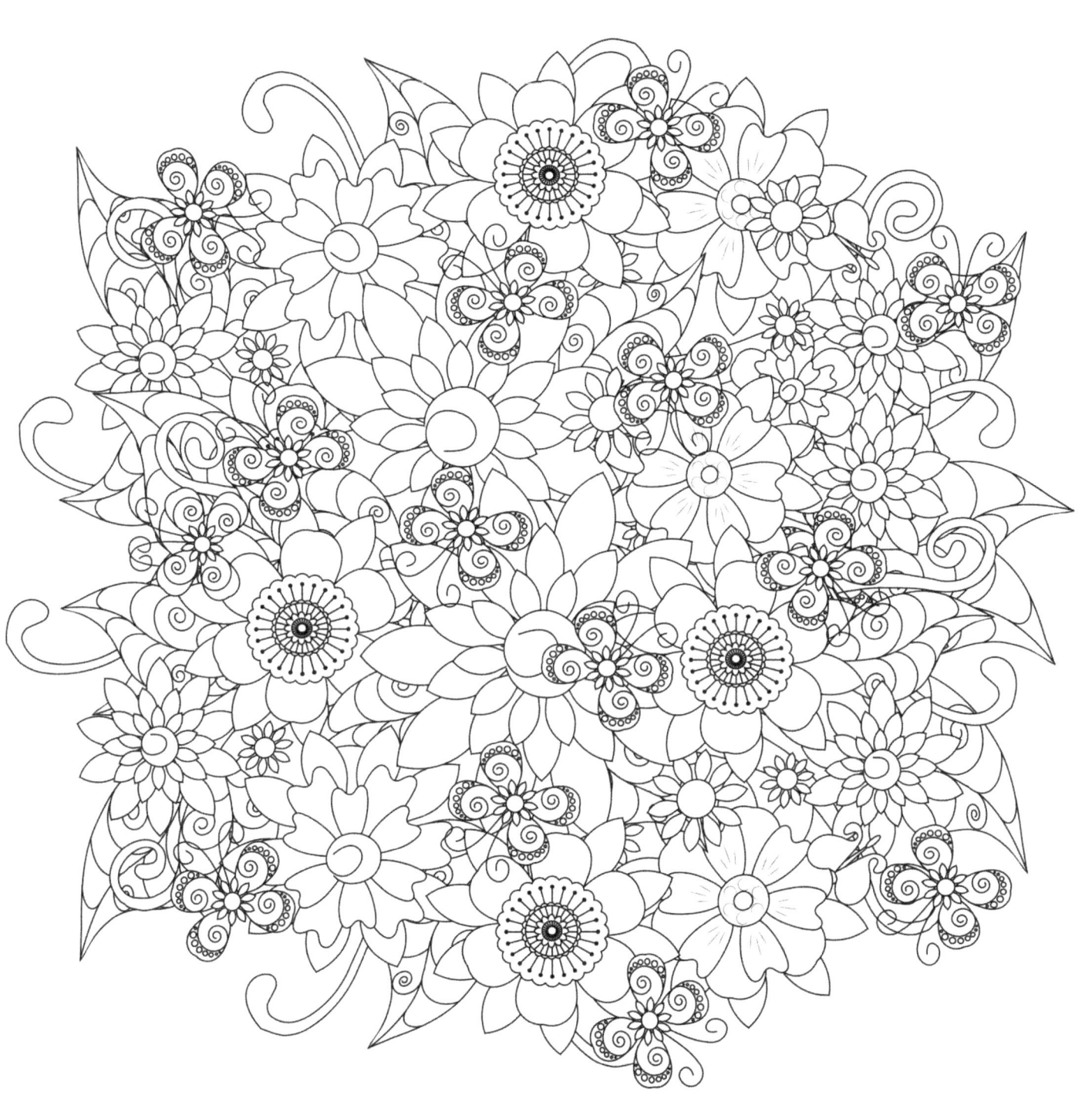

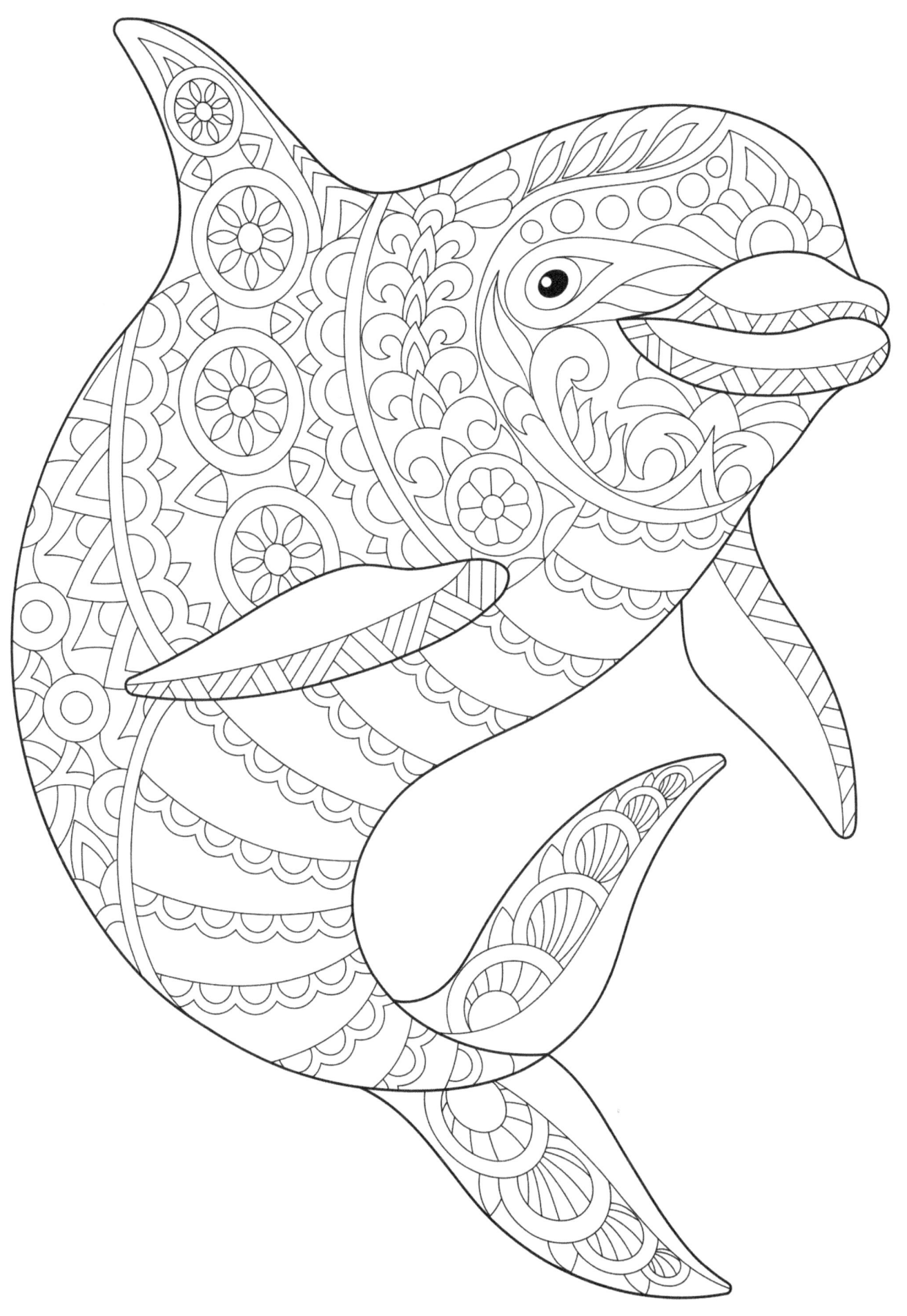

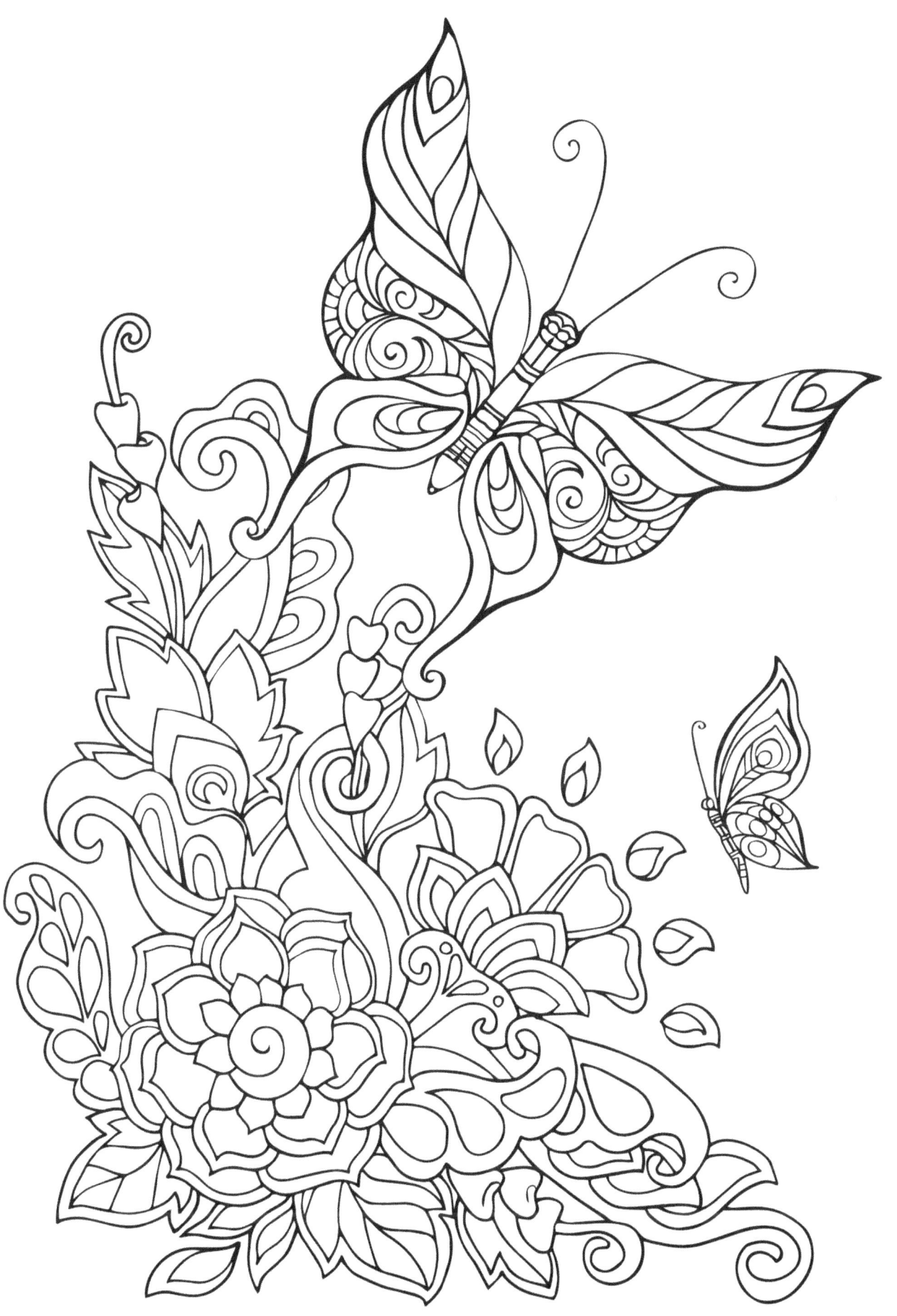

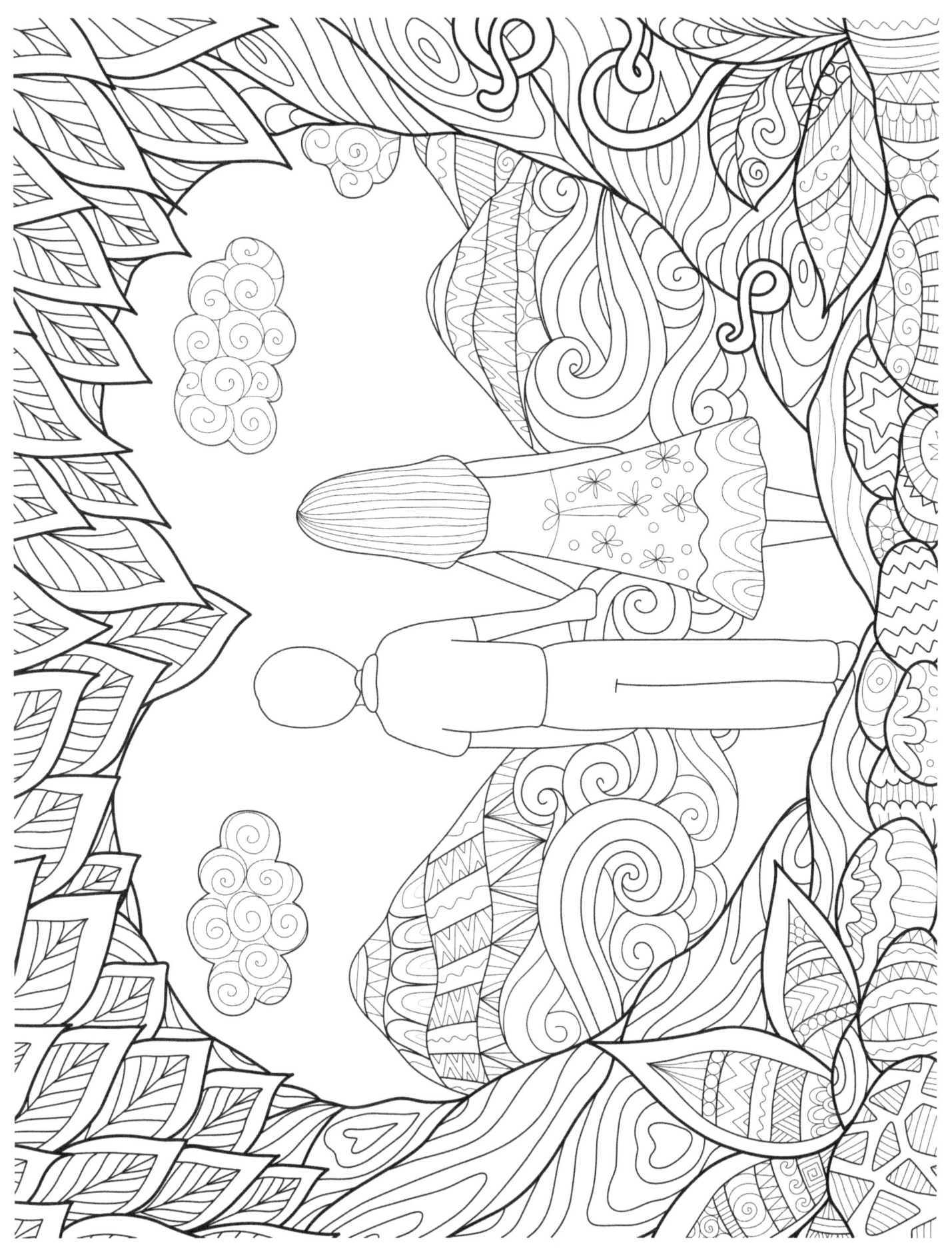

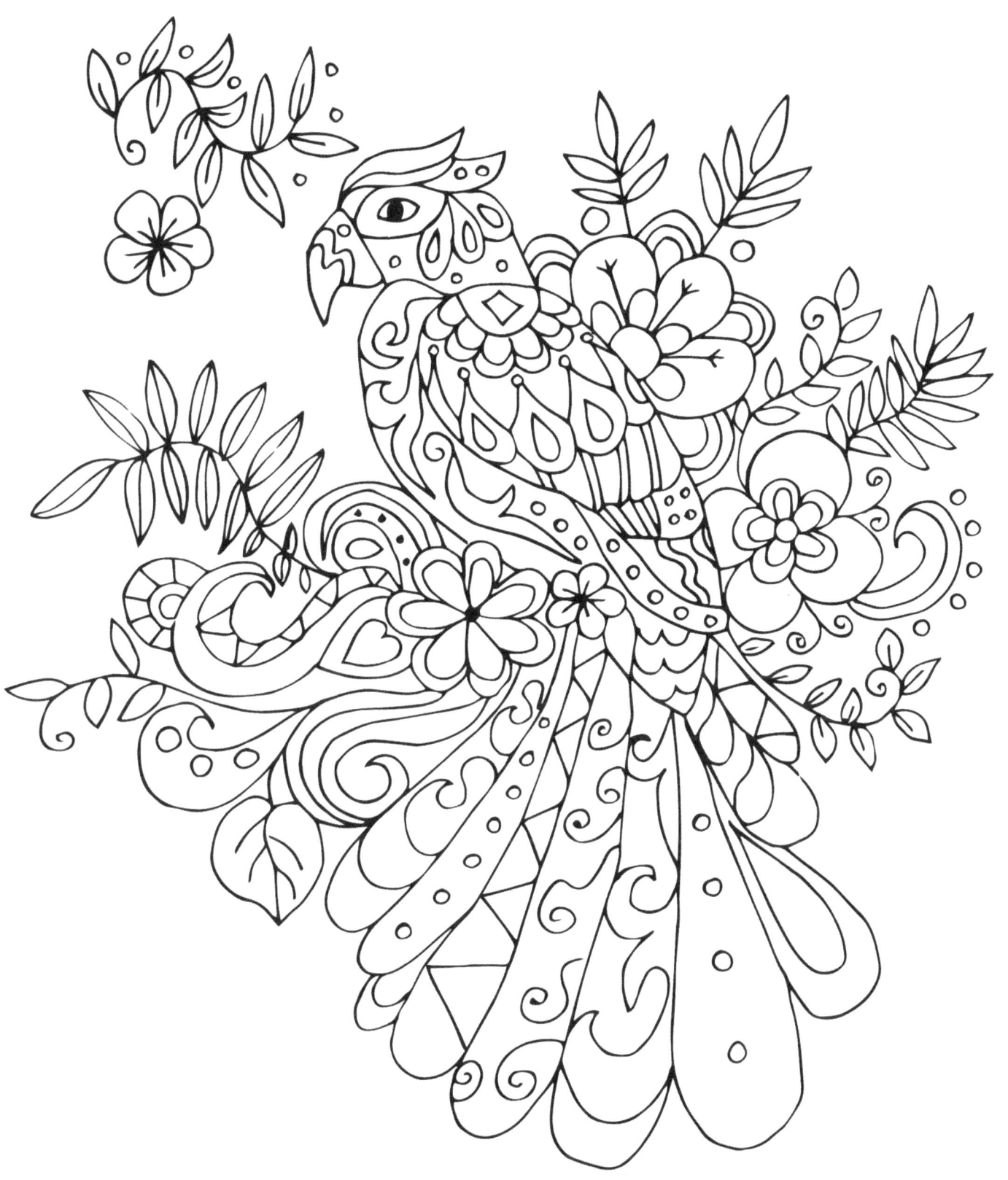

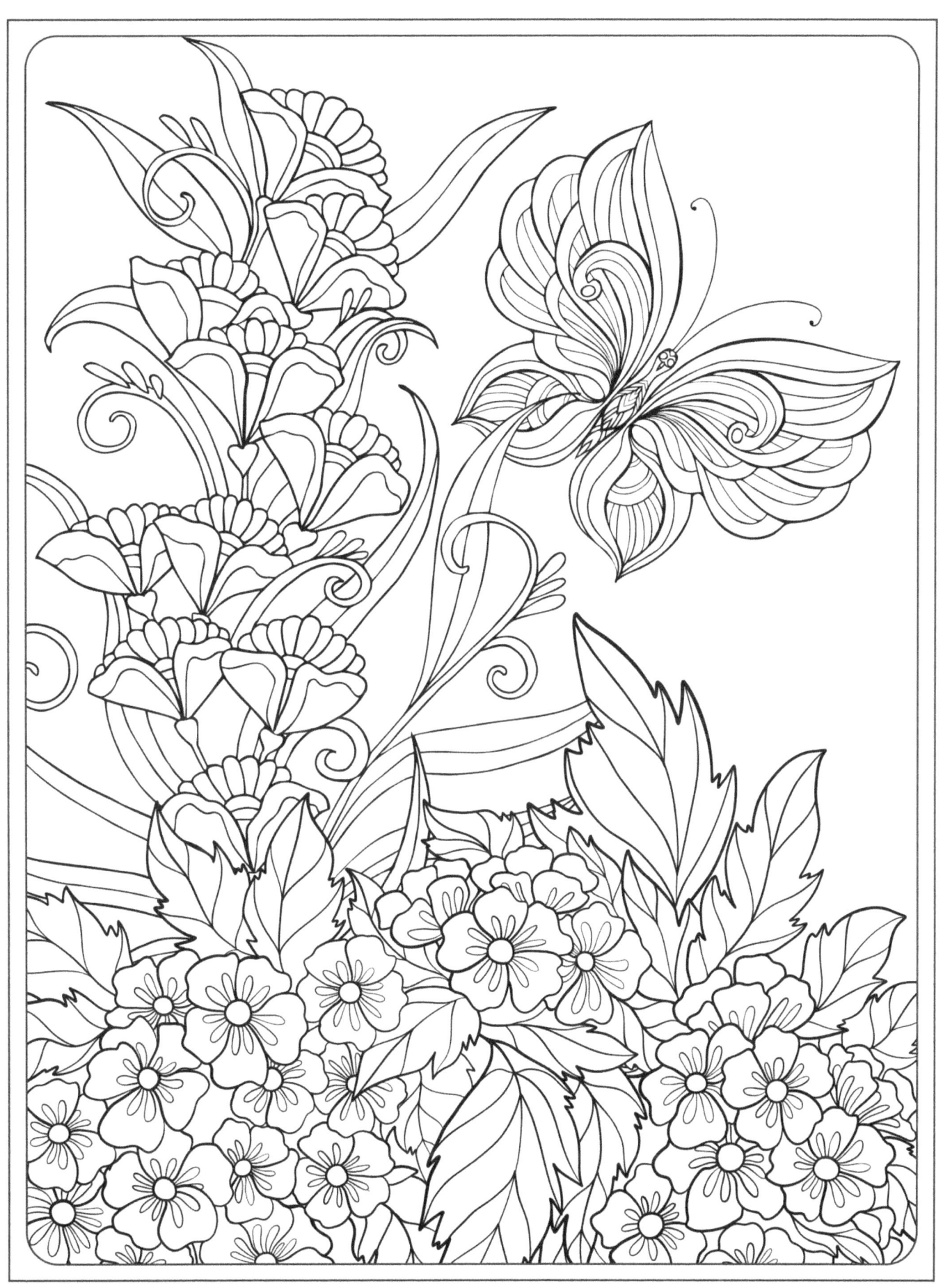

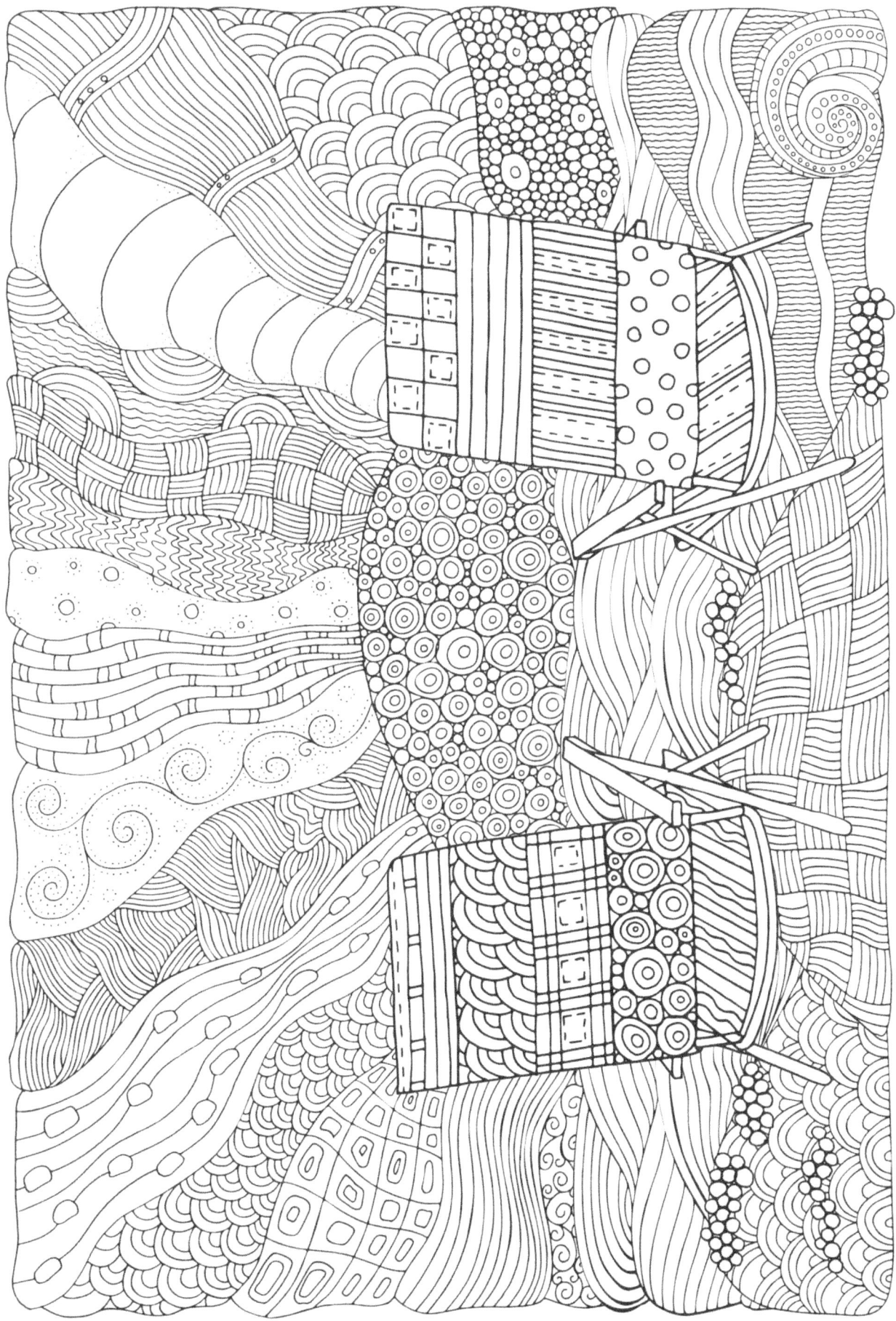

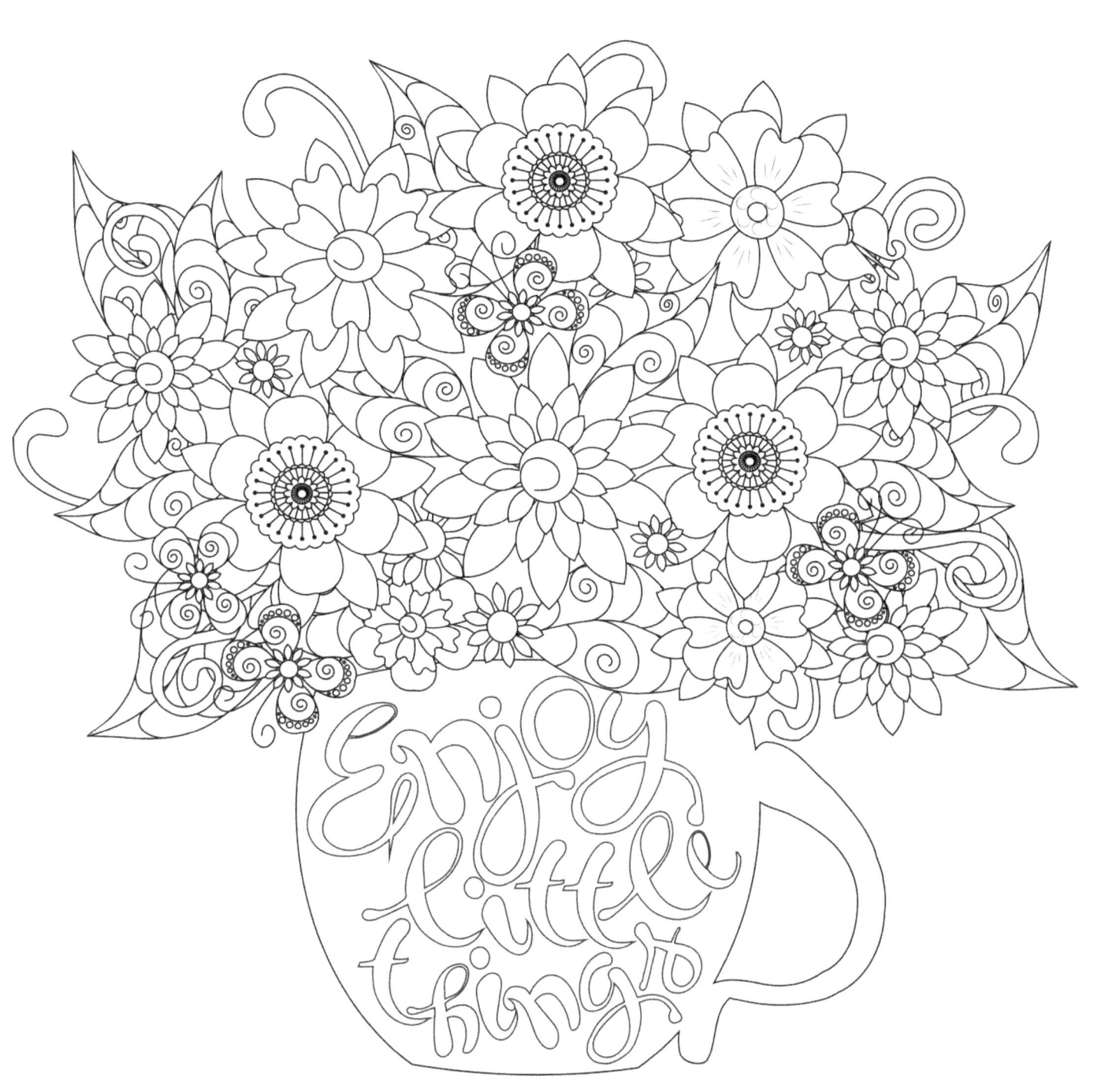

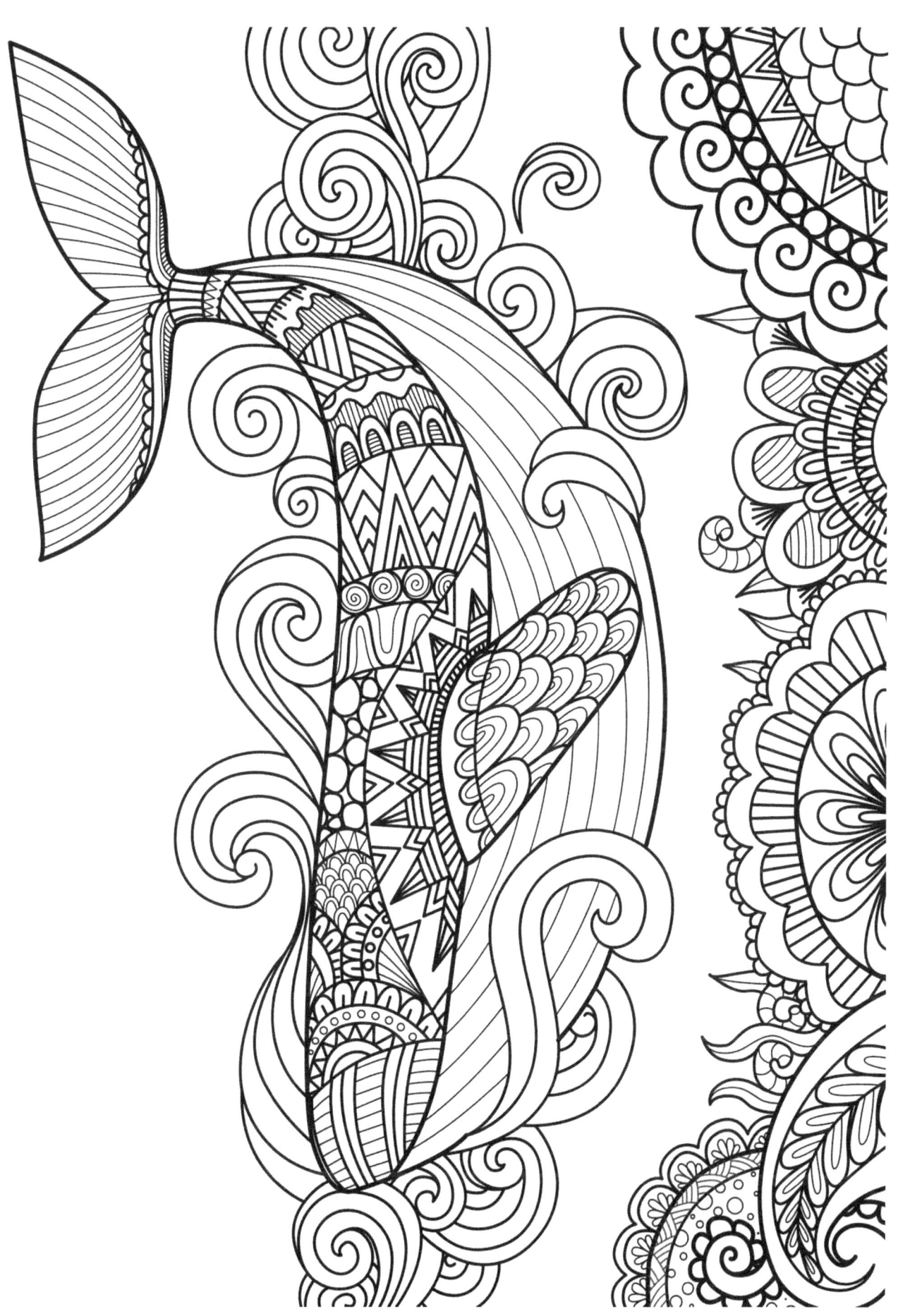

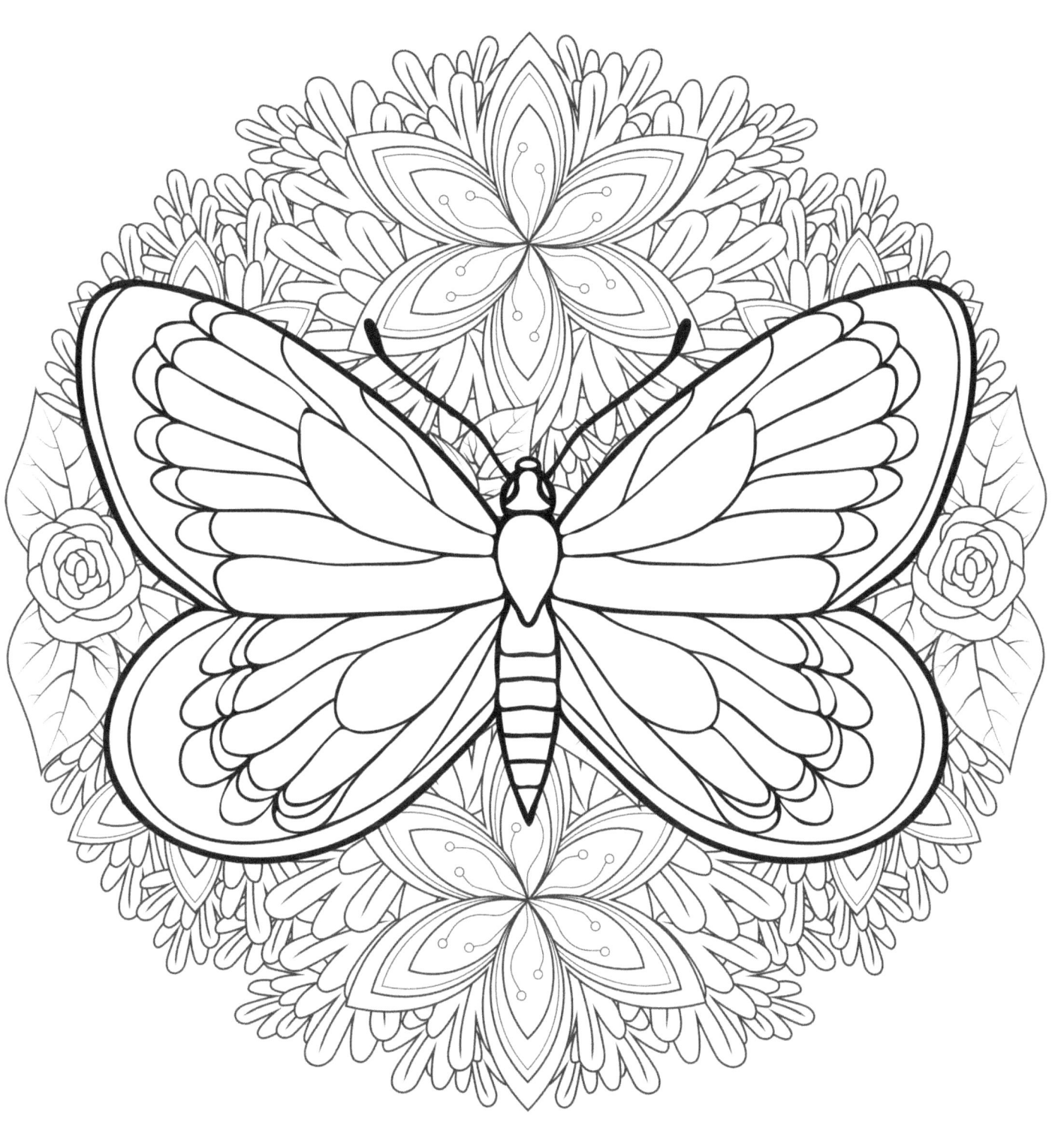

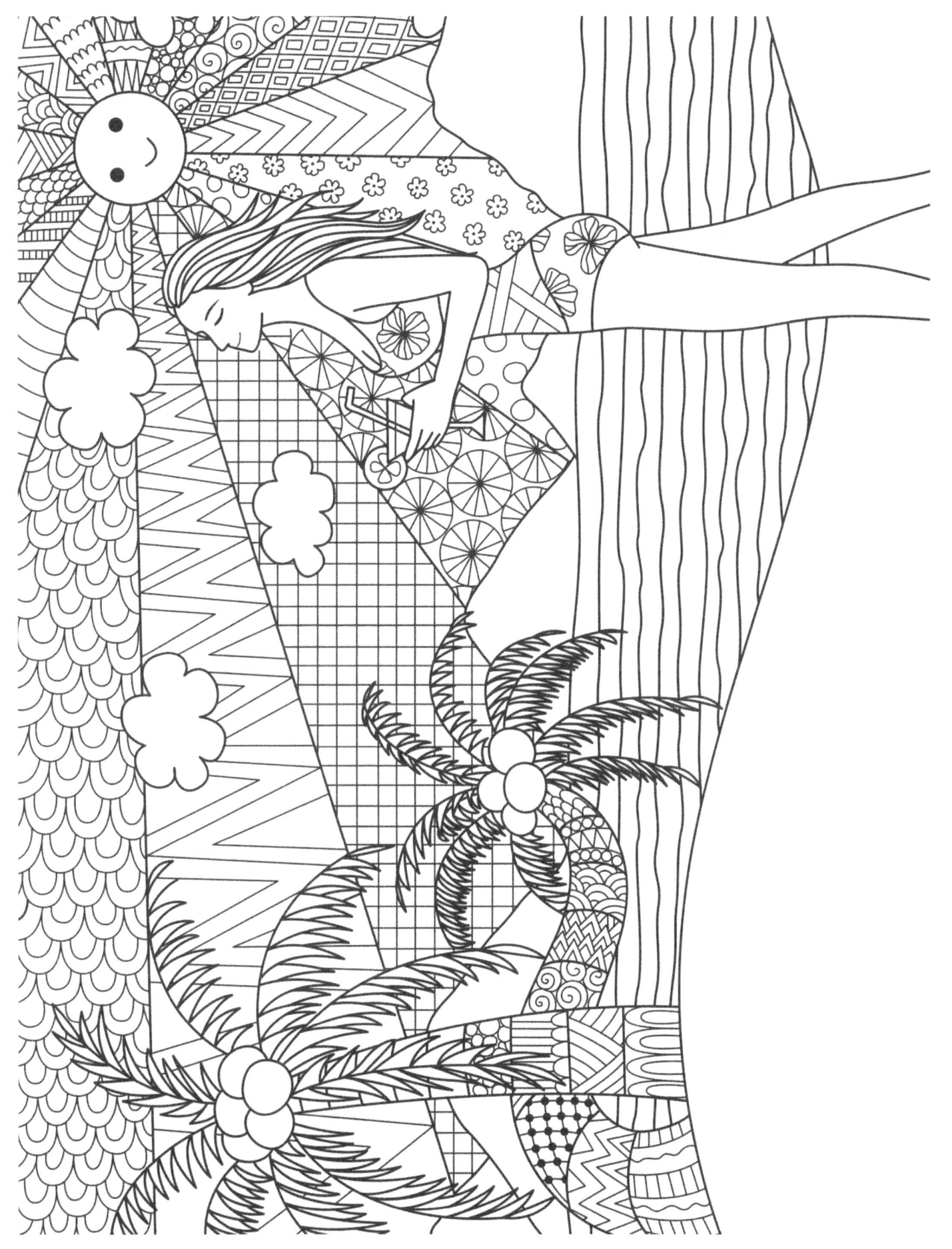

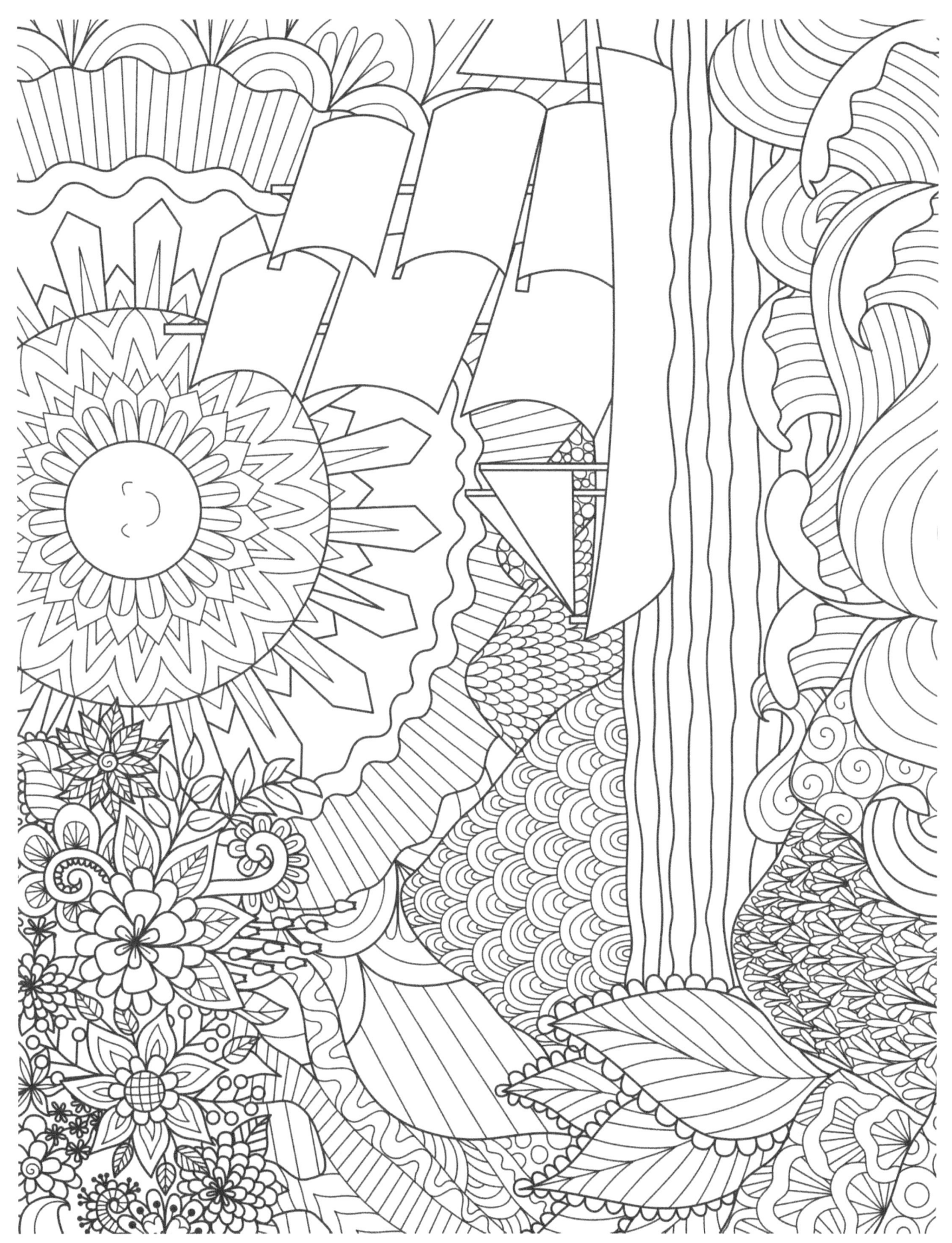

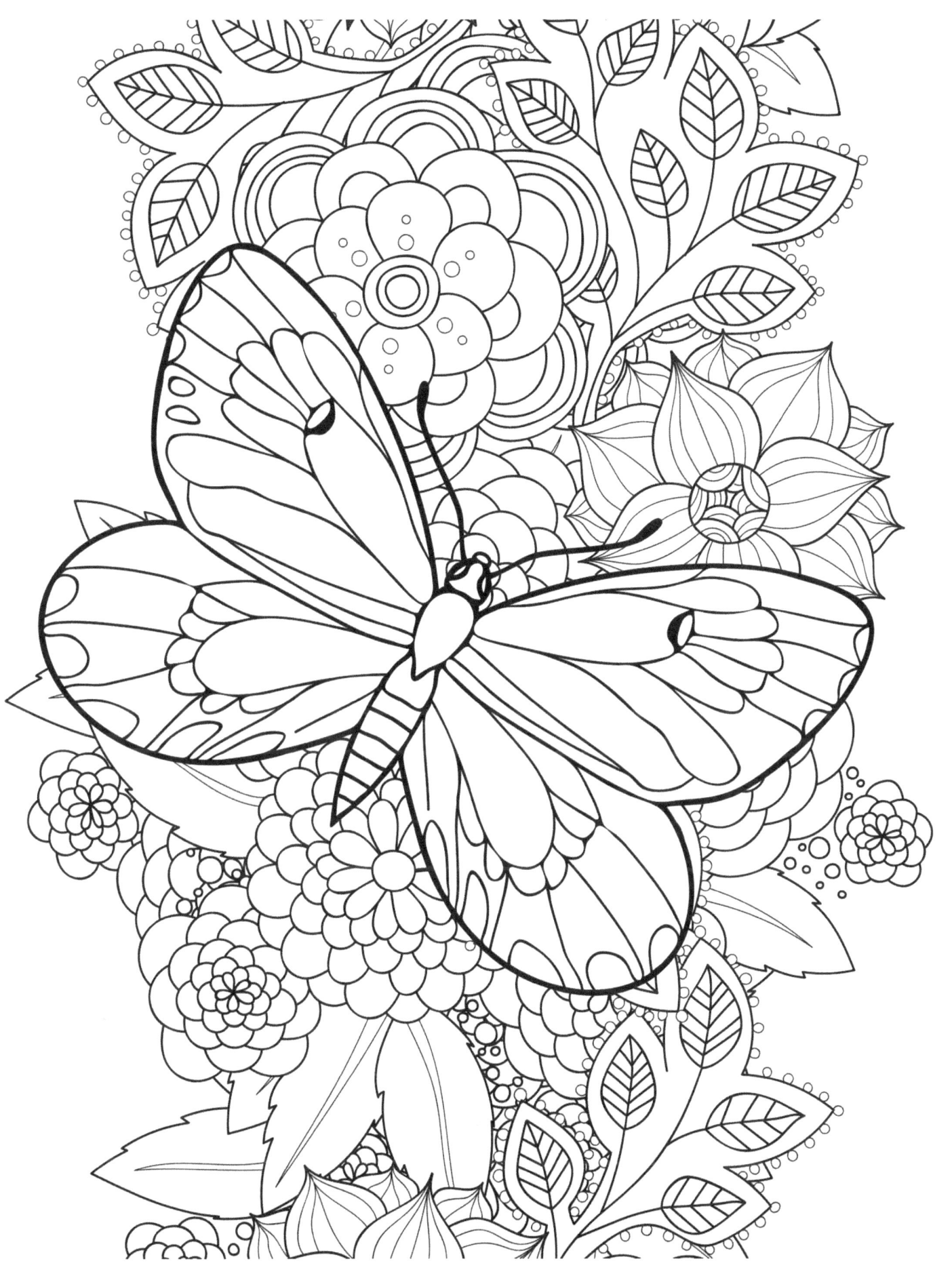

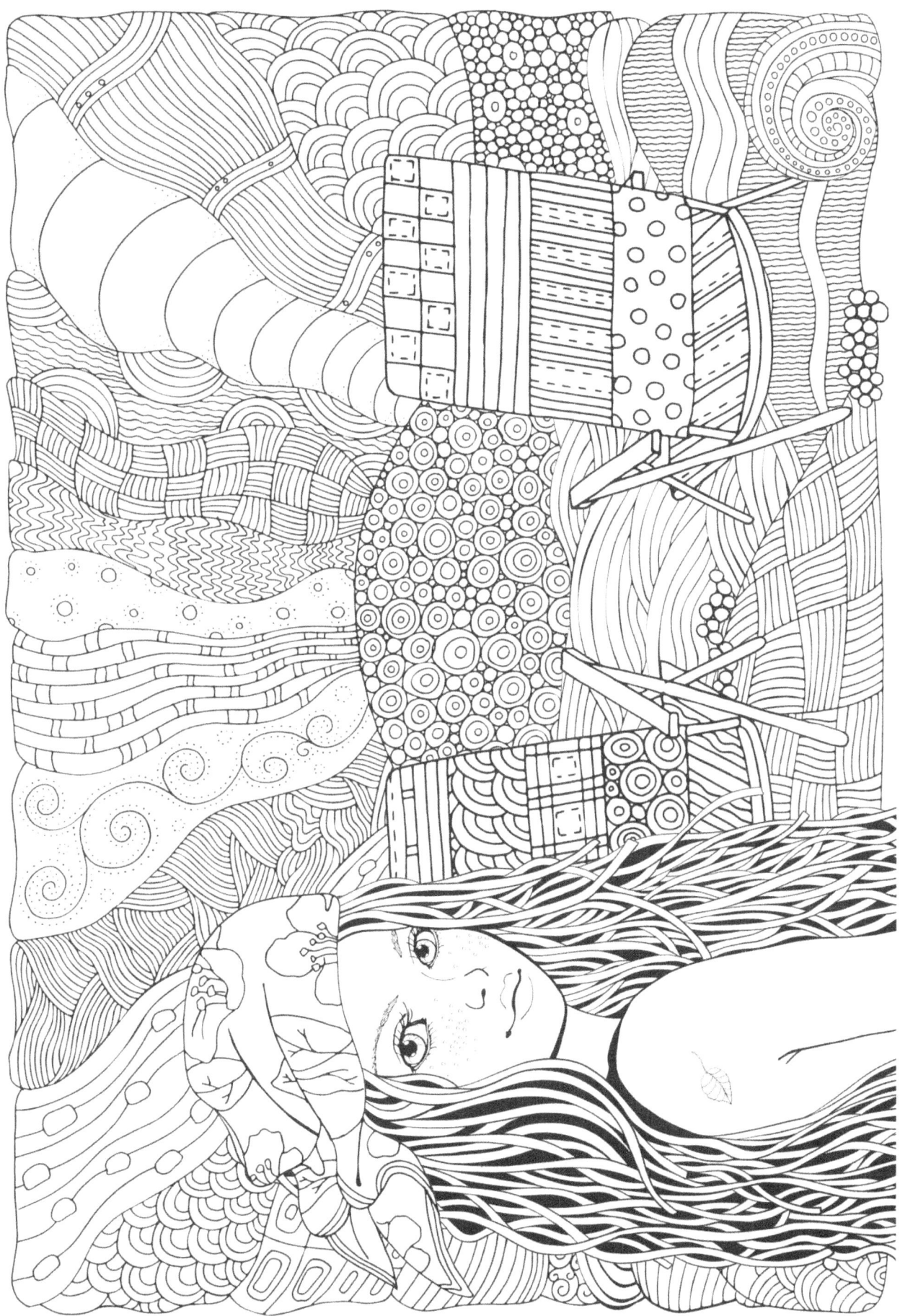

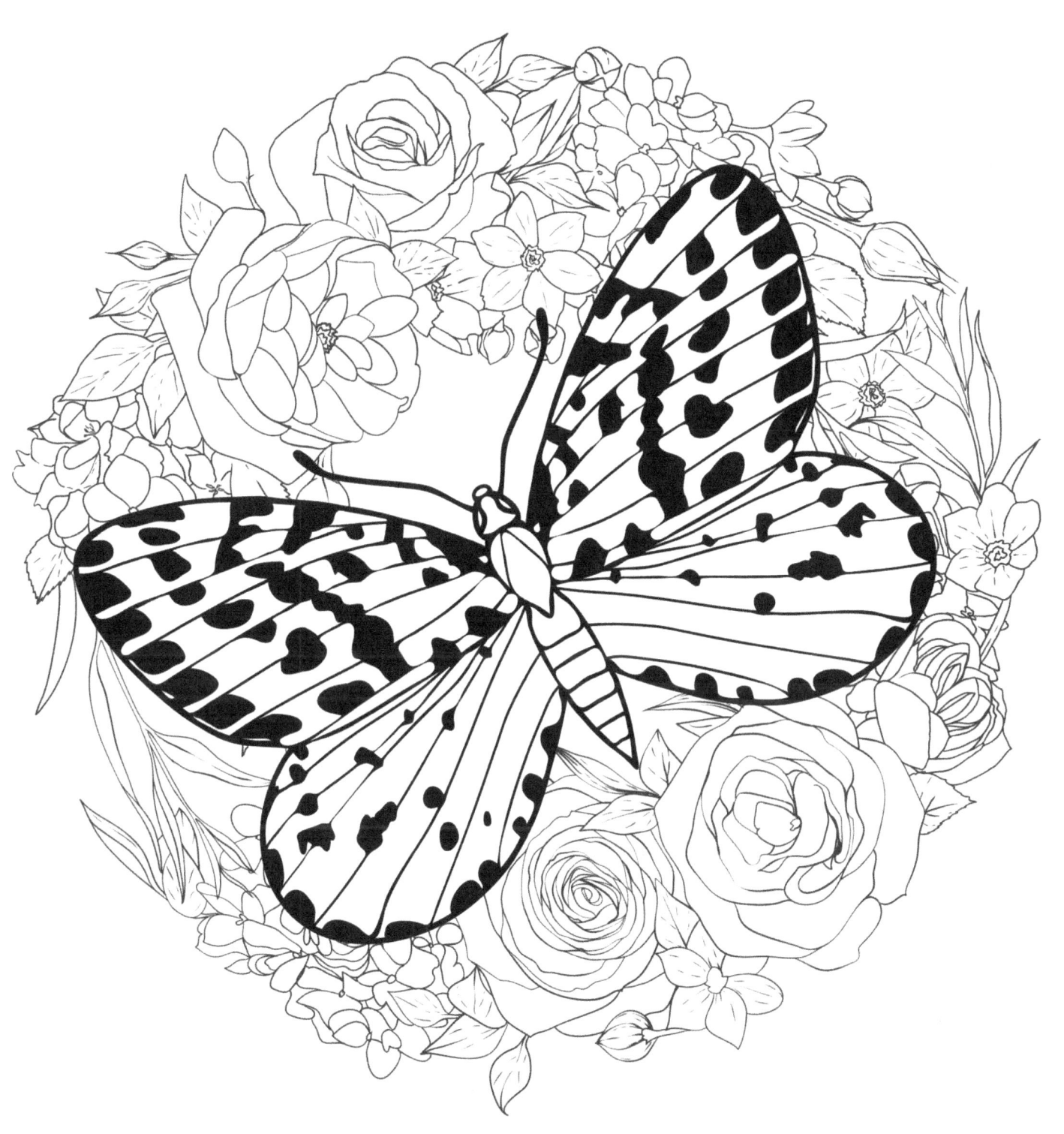

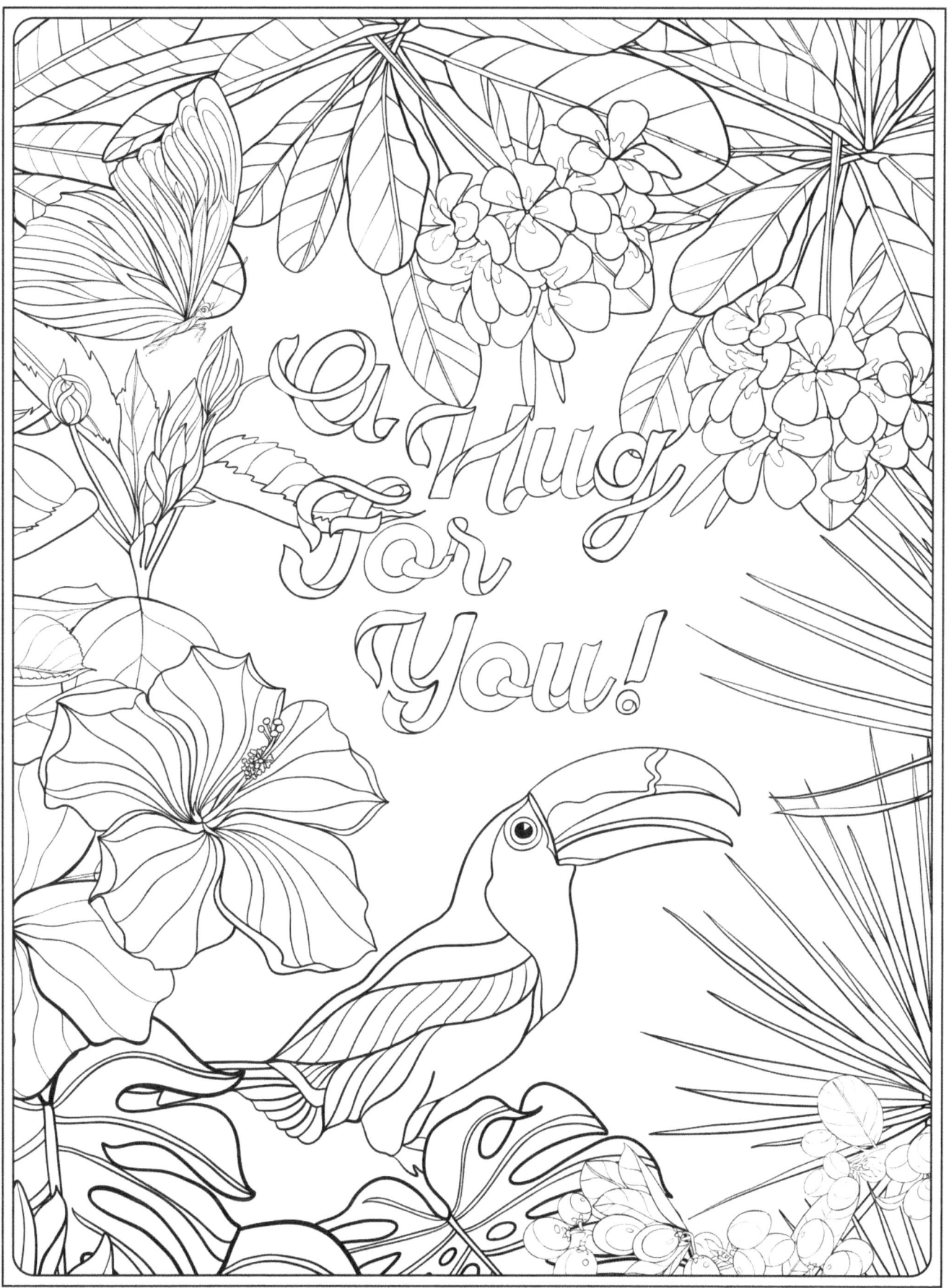

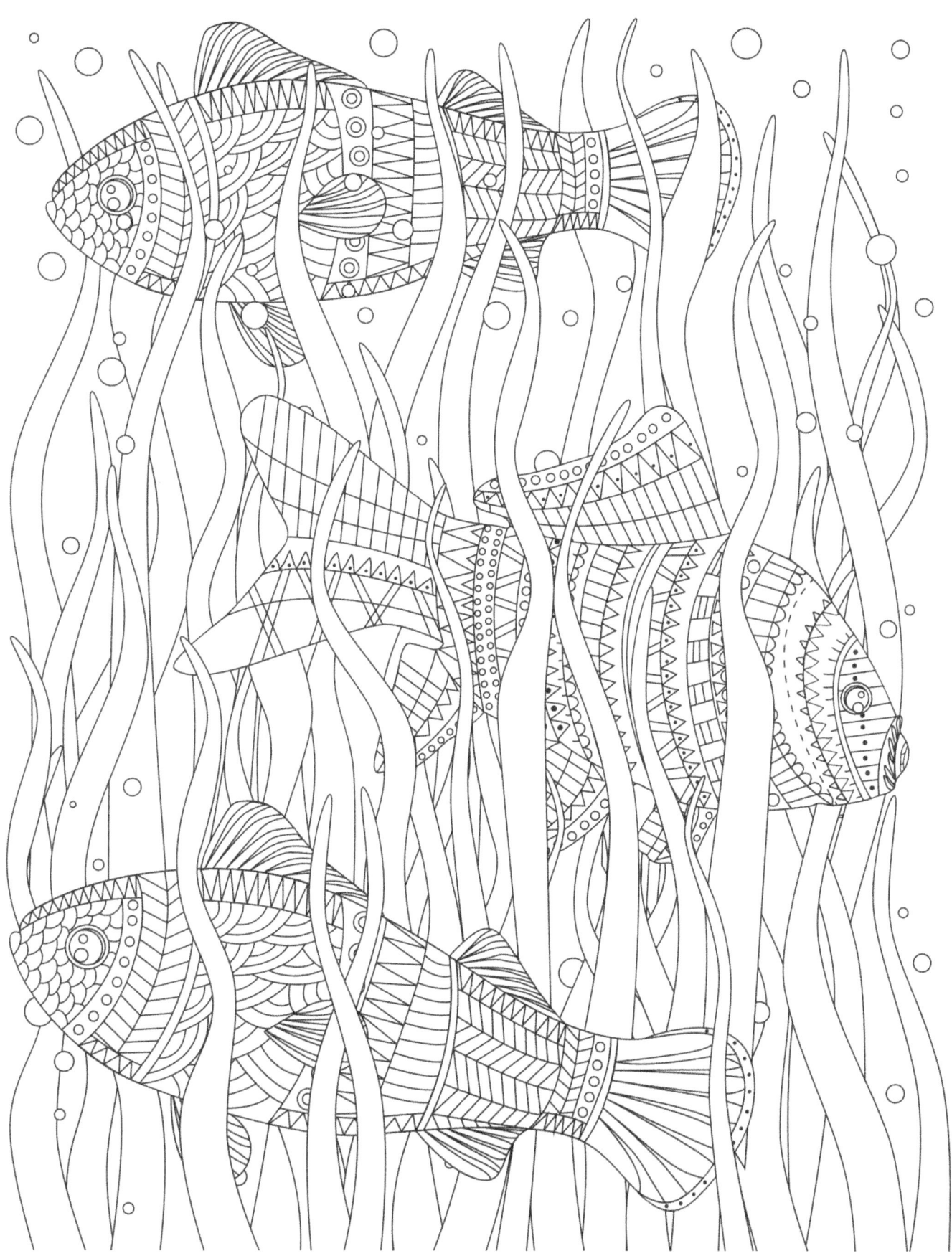

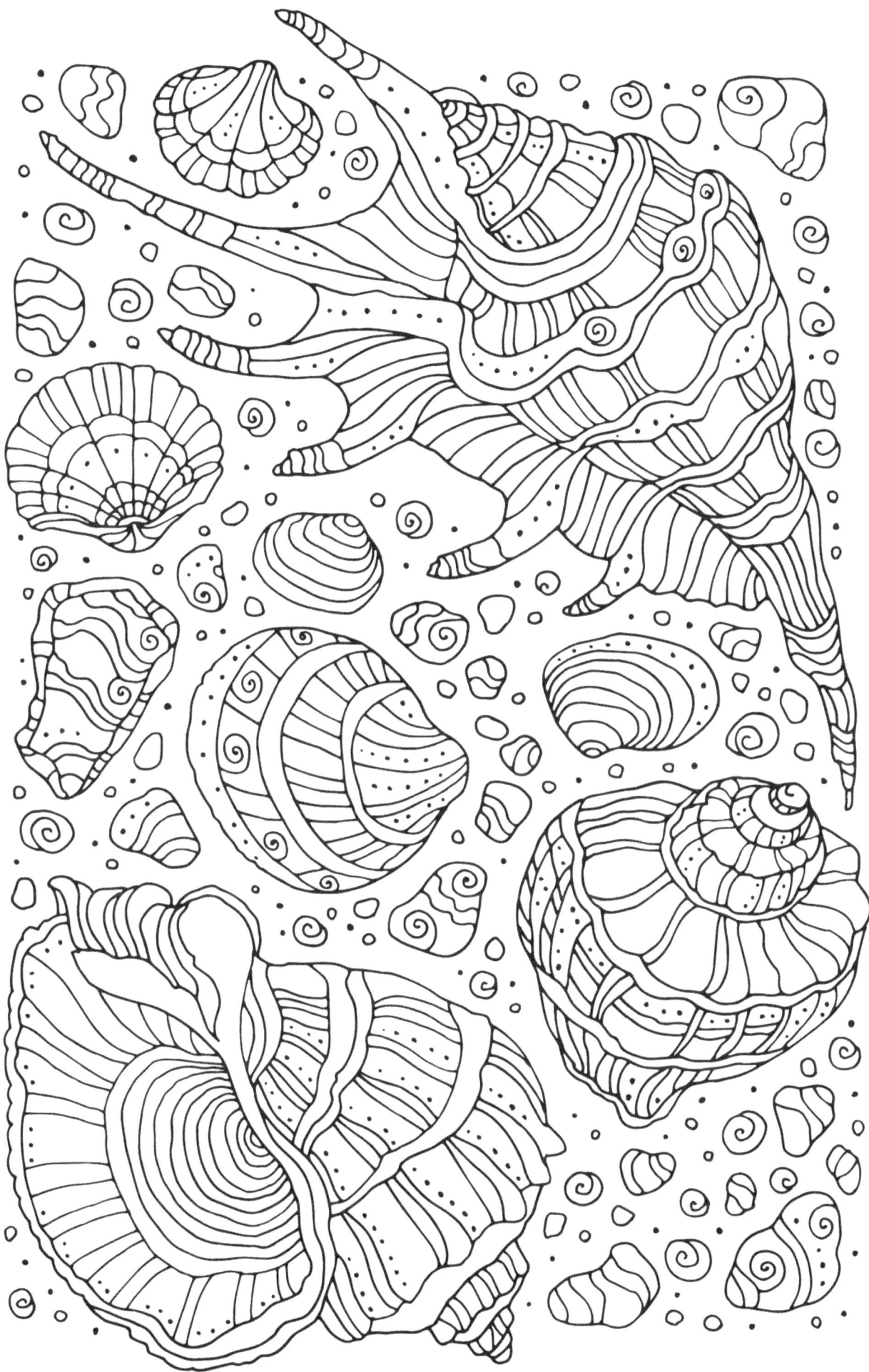

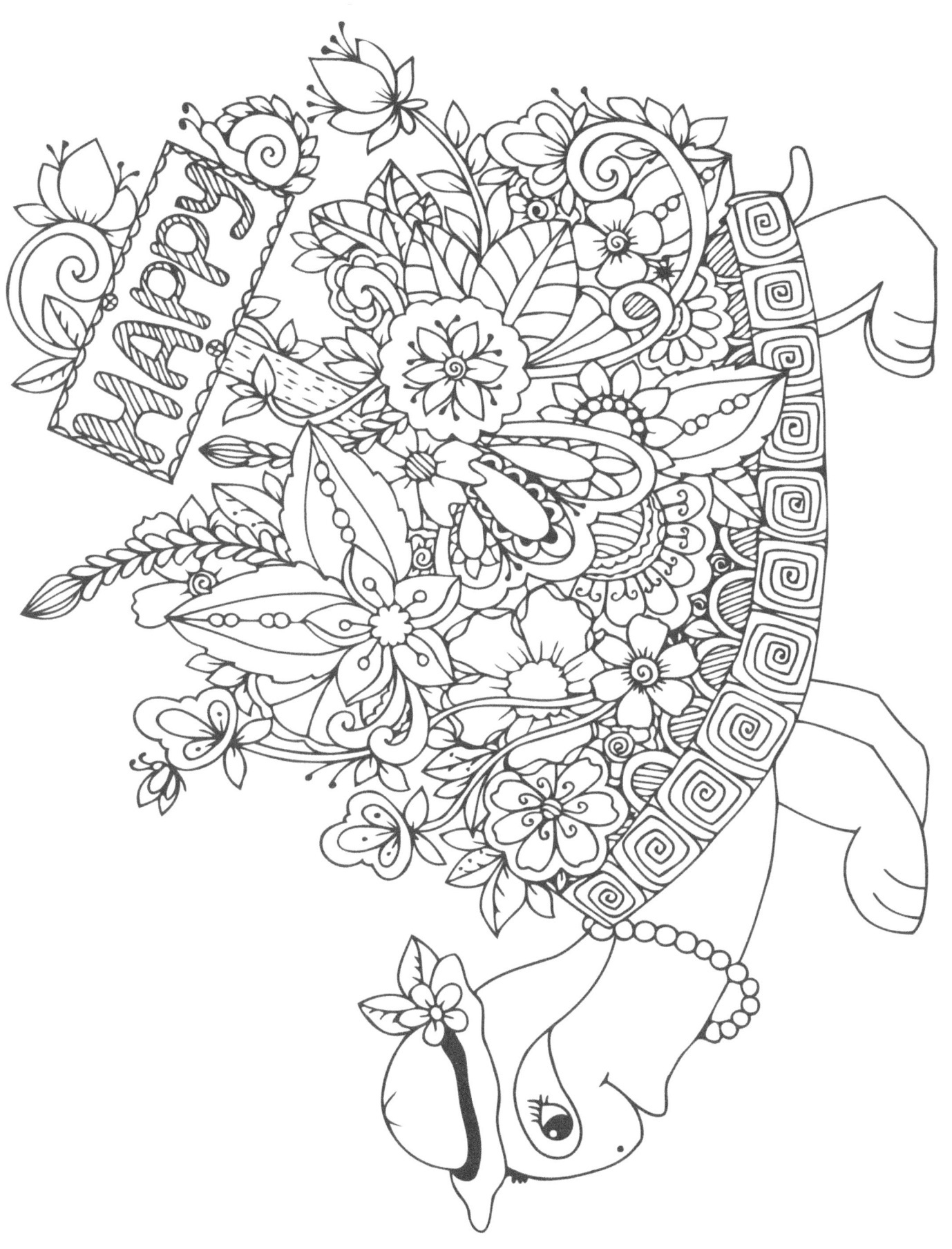

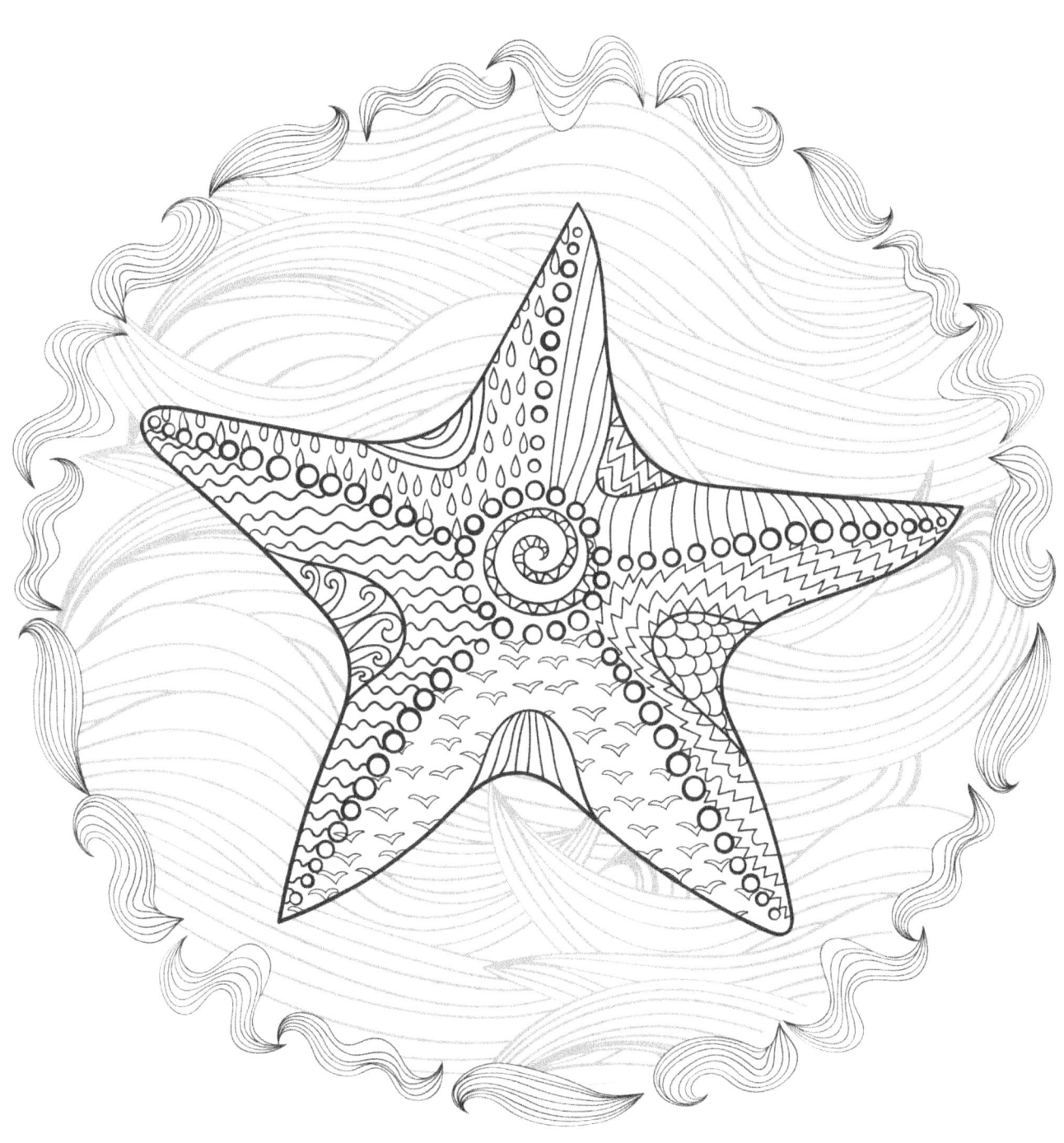

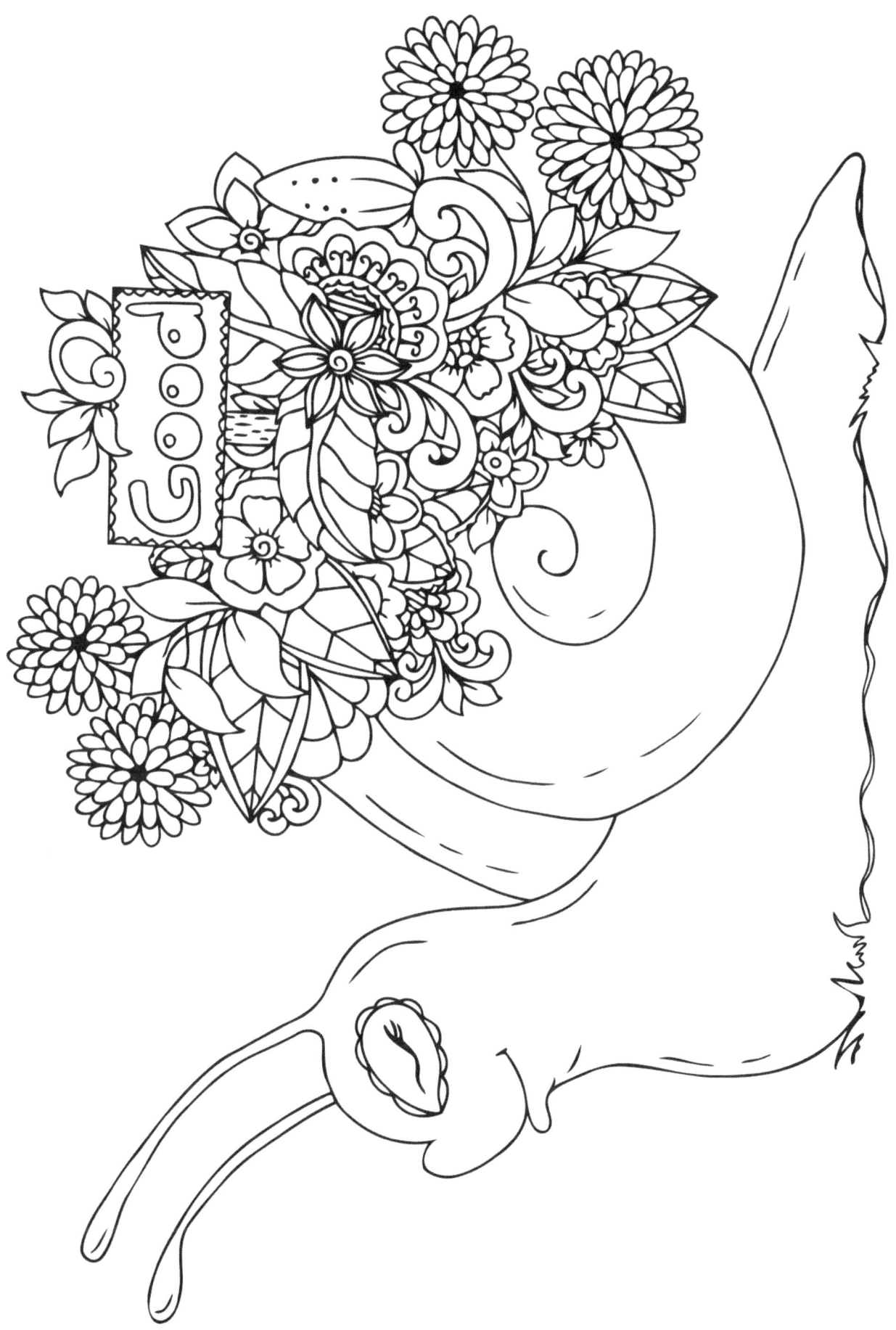

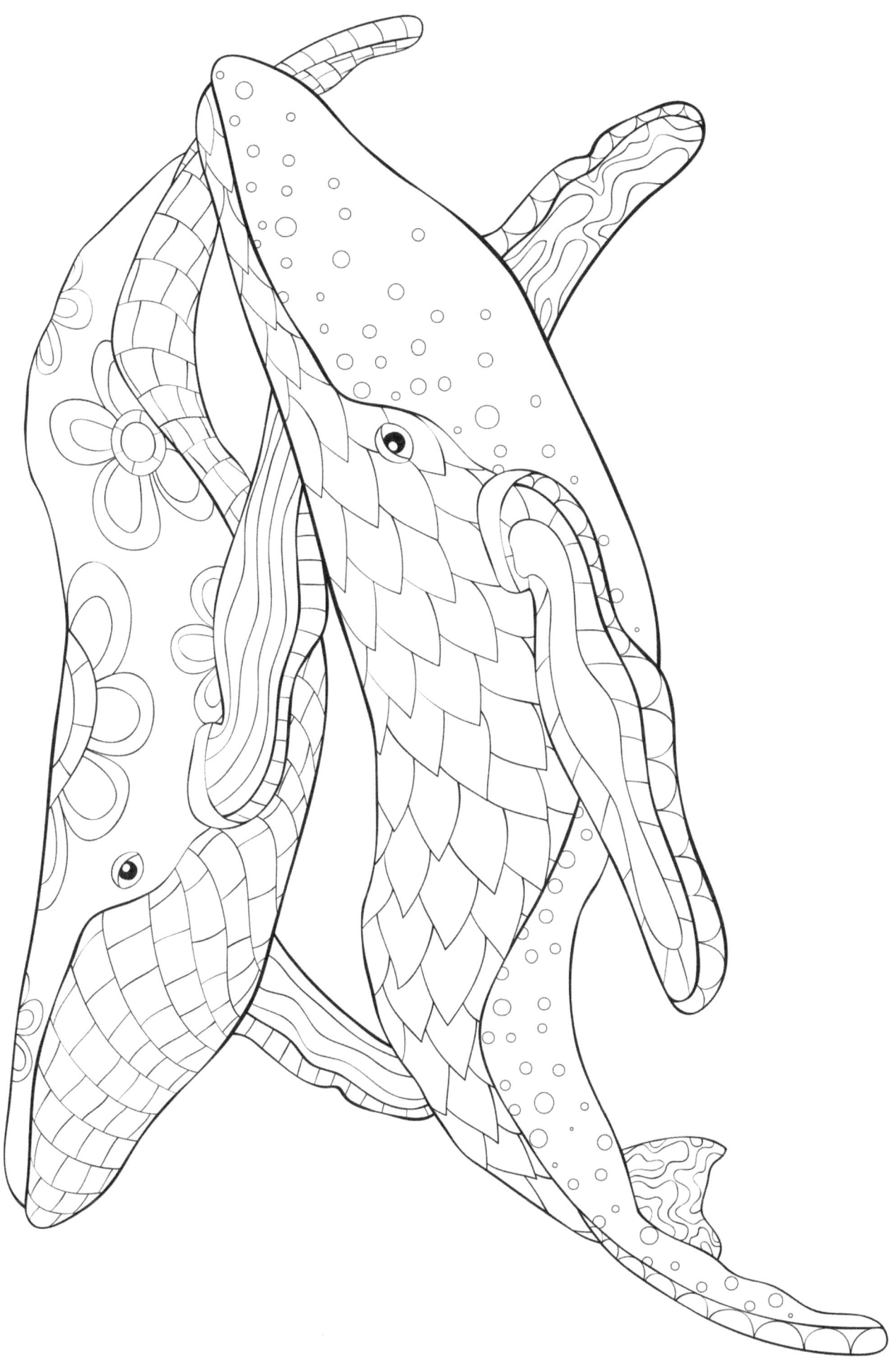

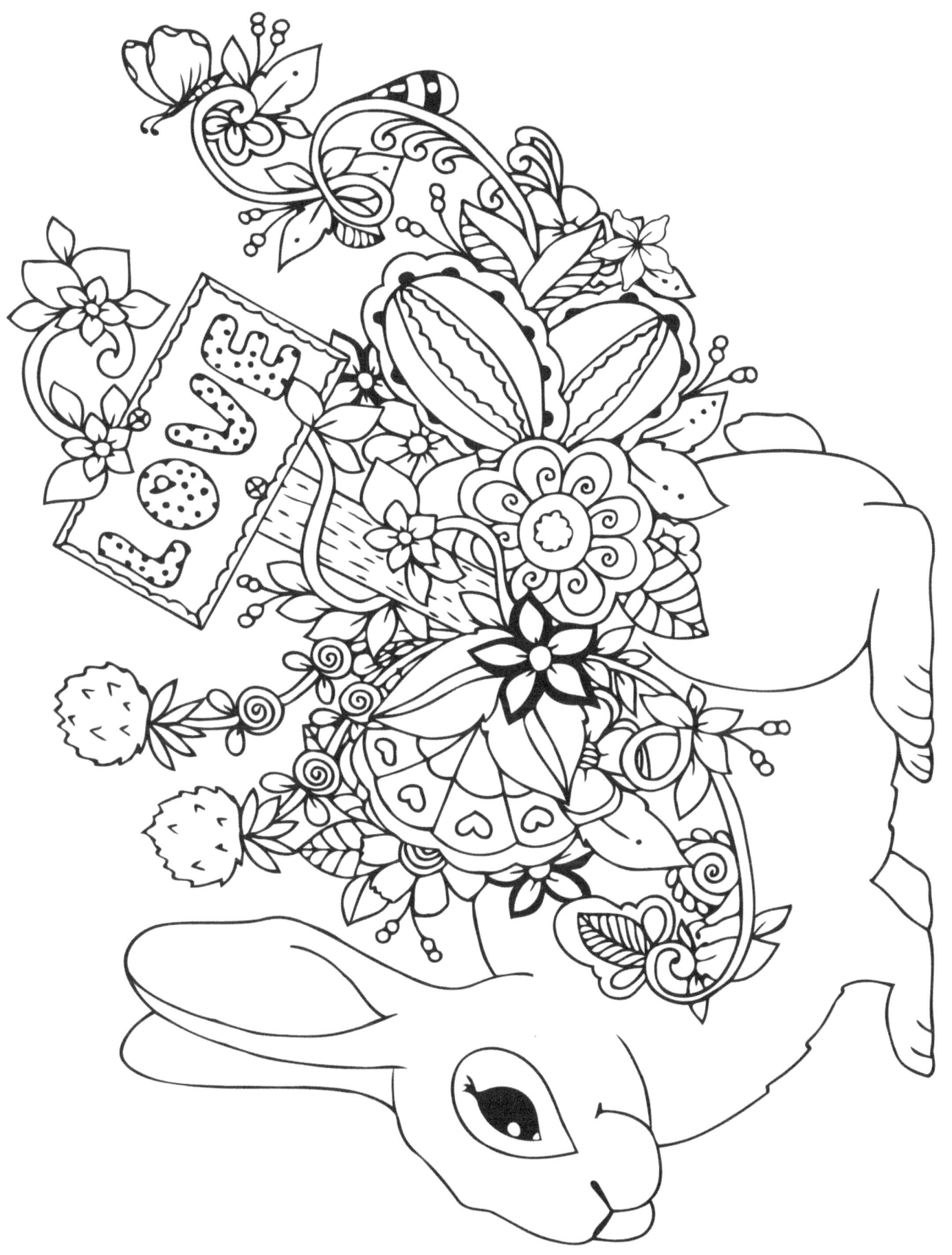

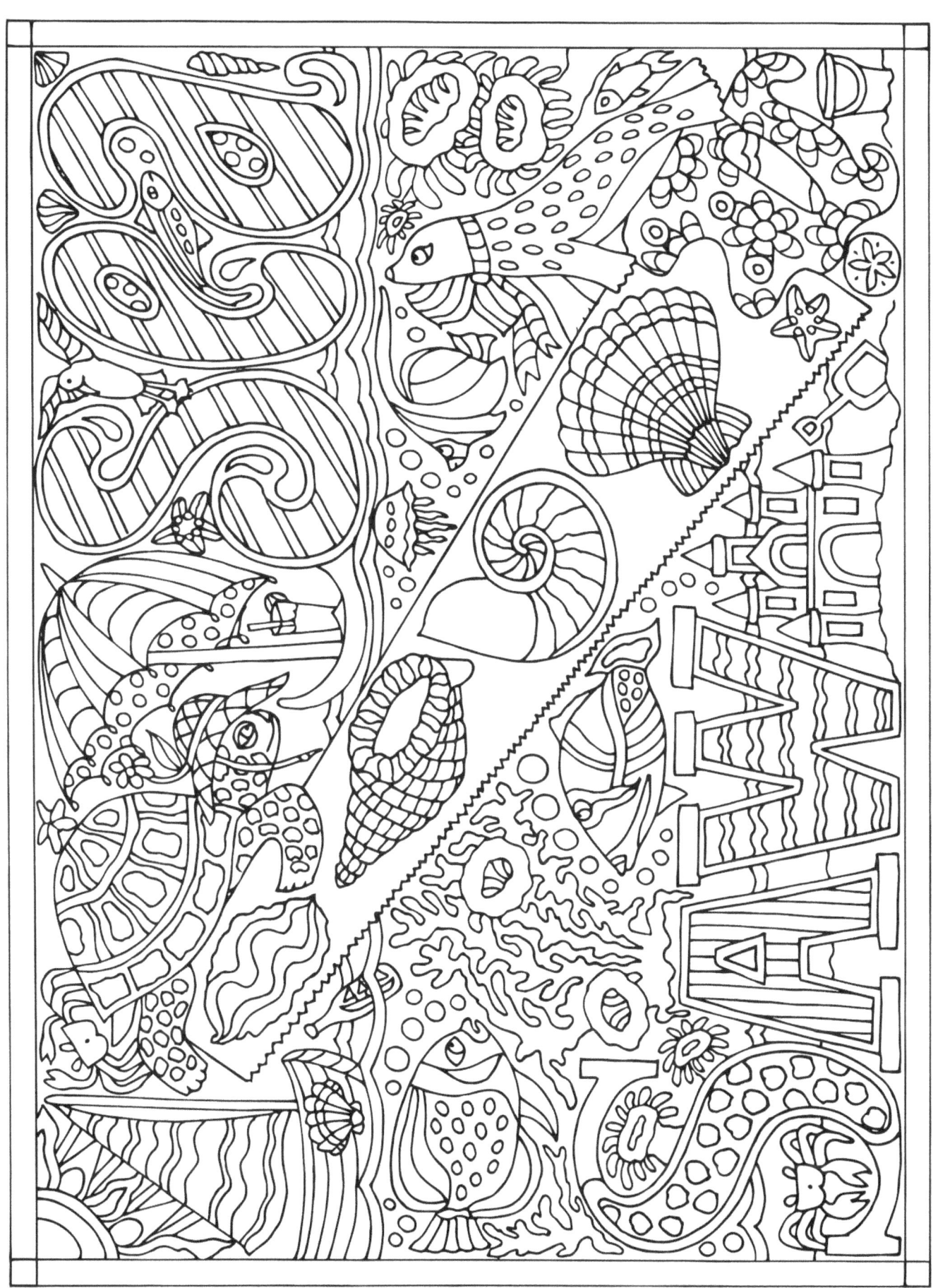

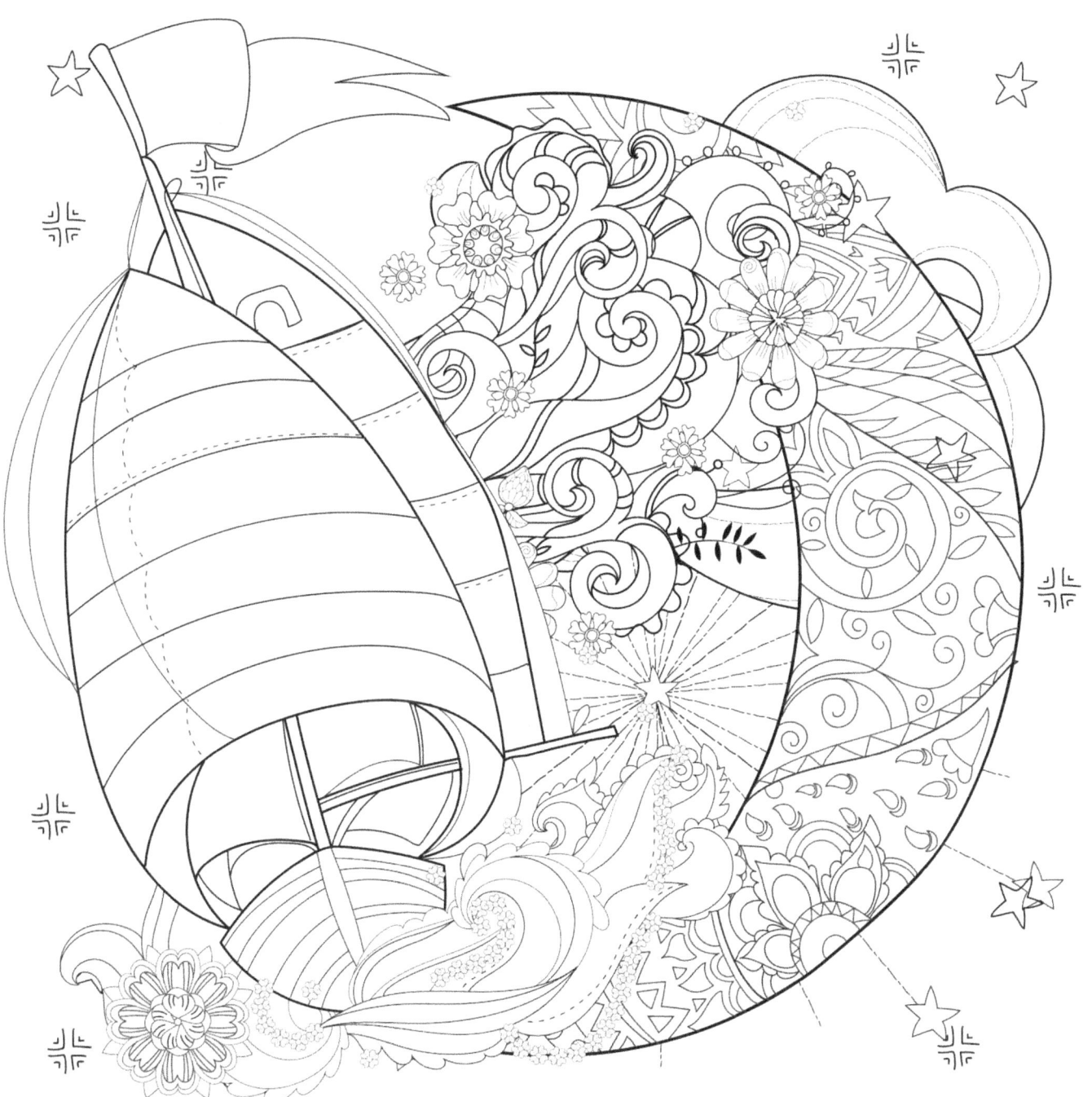

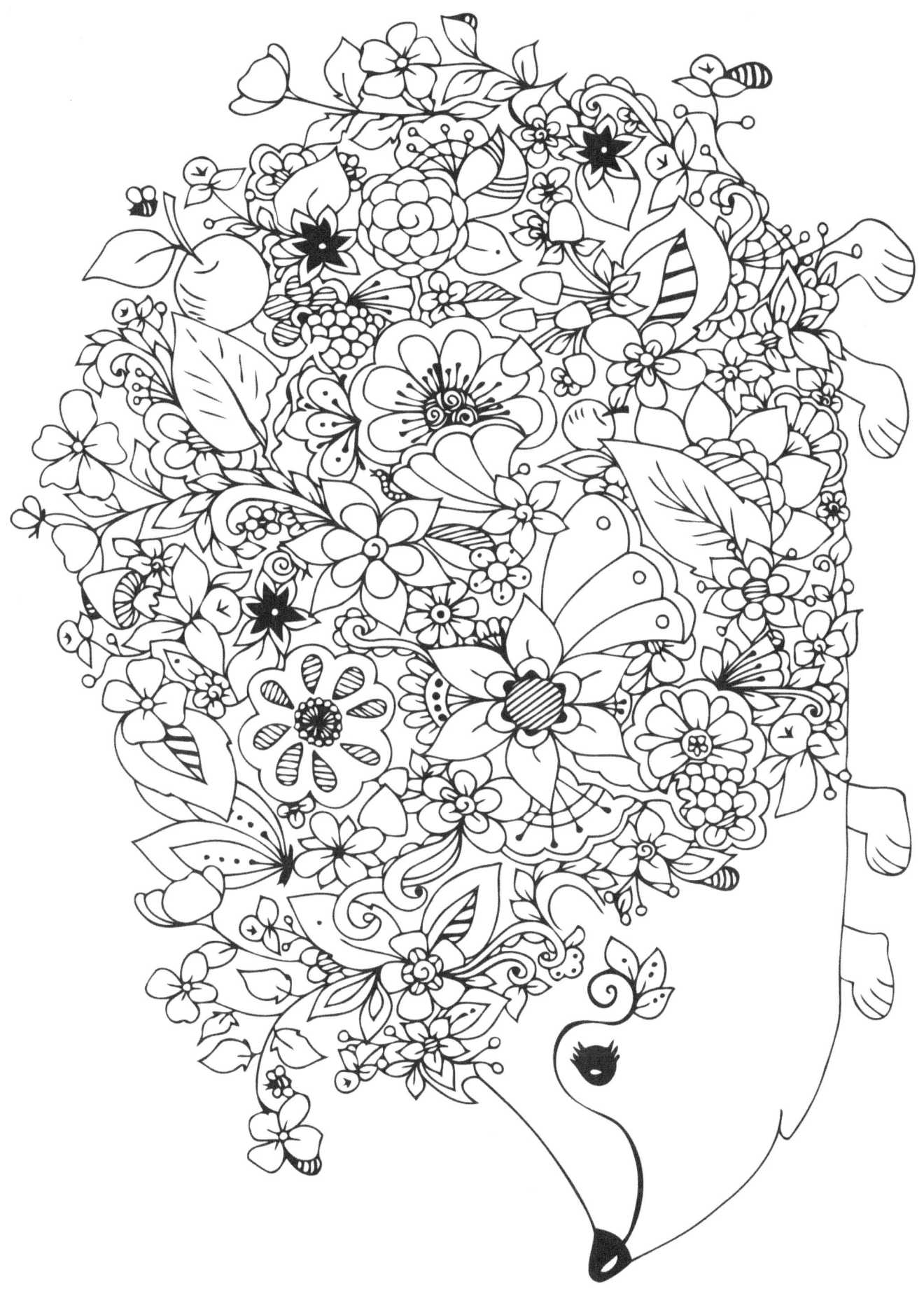

www.ingramcontent.com/pod-product-compliance
Lightning Source LLC
Chambersburg PA
CBHW081603280526
45788CB00011B/3536